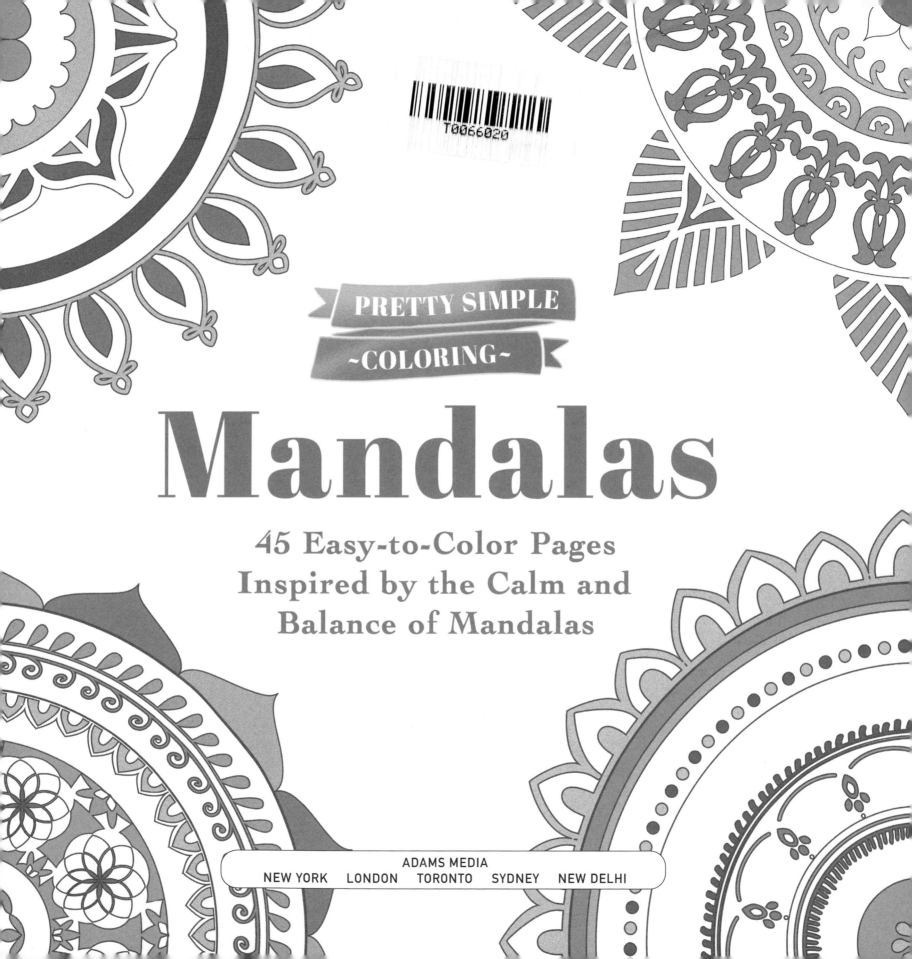

PRETTY SIMPLE

~COLORING~

Mandalas

45 Easy-to-Color Pages Inspired by the Calm and Balance of Mandalas

ADAMS MEDIA

NEW YORK   LONDON   TORONTO   SYDNEY   NEW DELHI

Adams Media
An Imprint of Simon & Schuster, Inc.
100 Technology Center Drive
Stoughton, Massachusetts 02072

First Adams Media trade paperback edition November 2023

ADAMS MEDIA and colophon are registered trademarks of Simon & Schuster, Inc.

For information about special discounts for bulk purchases, please contact Simon & Schuster Special Sales at 1-866-506-1949 or business@simonandschuster.com.

The Simon & Schuster Speakers Bureau can bring authors to your live event. For more information or to book an event, contact the Simon & Schuster Speakers Bureau at 1-866-248-3049 or visit our website at www.simonspeakers.com.

Interior images © iStockphoto.com; Getty Images; 123RF

Manufactured in the United States of America

10 9 8 7 6 5 4 3 2 1

ISBN 978-1-5072-2111-2

Contains material adapted from the following titles published by Adams Media, an Imprint of Simon & Schuster, Inc.: *The Big Book of Mandalas Coloring Book*, copyright © 2014, ISBN 978-1-4405-7986-8, and *The Big Book of Mandalas Coloring Book, Volume 2*, copyright © 2015, ISBN 978-1-4405-8625-5.

Introduction

Looking to do something creative, but don't have a lot of time?
Searching for an easy project to celebrate your inner peace?
Or maybe you're trying to find a new way to relax?
The answer is pretty simple.

Take out your colored pencils, pens, crayons, or markers, and get ready to be creative and relieve your stress with the forty-five lovely, easy-to-color images in *Pretty Simple Coloring: Mandalas*. The word "mandala" translates to "circle"; mandalas are often used as tools to promote relaxation. Each page in this book has a mandala that you can customize in the colors of your choosing. Unlike in other coloring books, these awesome images are designed with simple visual elements, which allow you to complete a page without a significant time commitment. And, because the art is easy to see with no complicated patterns, your eyes and hands will be less strained after your coloring sessions.

These easy, eye-catching designs also allow you to multitask if you want to. Color in a variety of different mandalas while you listen to your favorite podcast, catch up on a new show, or follow the narration of your latest audiobook. However you choose to color, you can take a deep breath and let your stress melt away as you clear your mind and work on these pretty simple coloring pages.

Let your inner artist inspire your color palette. Feel free to keep your preferred colors close to the peaceful blues, greens, and purples on the cool end of the color spectrum. Or take the liberty to create electrifying mandalas with warm reds, oranges, and yellows. Let the pencils, pens, crayons, or markers inspire your hand, and personalize these gorgeous patterns as you see fit.

So whether you want to use this book's mandalas to relax and open your mind, or you just want a stress-free way to color, it's time to dive into these simple, quick, and beautiful pages, and get coloring.

Image © Getty Images/kostenkodesign

MAKE THE MOST OF YOUR FREE TIME!

PRETTY SIMPLE

~COLORING~

Nature Scenes

45 Easy-to-Color Pages
Inspired by the Beauty
of Nature

Pick Up Your Copy Today!

adamsmedia
An Imprint of Simon & Schuster
A Paramount Company